#UWon tStarve:
Key Principles for
Entrepreneur
Development

By: J Haleem

Limits of Liability and Disclaimer of Warranty

The author and publisher shall not be liable for your misuse of this material. This book is strictly for informational and educational purposes.

Warning – Disclaimer

The purpose of this book is to educate and entertain. The author and/or publisher do not guarantee that anyone following these techniques, suggestions, tips, ideas, or strategies will become successful. The author and/or publisher shall have neither liability nor responsibility to anyone concerning any loss or damage caused, or alleged to be caused, directly or indirectly by the information contained in this book.

TABLE OF CONTENTS

DEDICATION

To my aspiring entrepreneurs, this book is dedicated to you. May you enjoy all the success life has to offer.

INTRODUCTION

When I decided to write *U Won't Starve: Key Principles for Entrepreneur Development*, I knew I wanted it to be easy-to-read, so whether you are in business or not, you can still understand it and get something out of it. In this book, you will find answers to your most pressing questions, practical examples and step-by-step processes to walk you through your business's most pressing concerns.

As I've been learning more about myself and investing in personal development, I have spent a lot of my time reading and studying. My studies indicate that most of us are of the mindset that entrepreneurship is not a skill. I beg to differ. If something isn't working, true entrepreneurs are able to pivot and make adjustments - they have the ability to stop one thing and move on to another.

And so, this *is* a skill. This is a vocation. Reaching a level of entrepreneurial mastery is what gave me this platform to stand on. The true essence of this book is to debunk some of the myths that people have with becoming a business owner.

When I made the decision to leave my $8/hour job, after only working for one year in 2014, it was because I knew I was destined for more - that I *was* more and while I was tired of the space I was in, I knew I couldn't move too quickly. You see, I'm always calculated. Prior to making this decision, I began to hustle while I work, the first principle of #IWontStarve.

In this book, each principle is broken down and explained in detail. Those principles are described below.

1. Hustle While You Work
2. Market Research
3. Doing Business on Your Own Level
4. Networking
5. Strategic Partnerships/Alliances

At the time that this book is being written, the world is living through a global pandemic, COVID-19, also known as the Coronavirus. These are unprecedented times that took the world by storm. No one was prepared for it. In fact, much of our country dismissed the seriousness. As a result, many businesses have been shut down, and individuals have lost their jobs, schools are closed and that is only the front end. We have no idea, at least at the time this book is being released - of exactly what the long-term ramifications will be.

While this is new, I've been here before, I've lived through two prior crises, (The Great Recession of 2010 and the 1,000-year Historic Flood in 2015), now, currently living through a third - comfortably because I was determined I won't starve. Now, I pass the baton to you. I believe that once you complete this book, you too will have the same mindset. 20 years later, here I stand a successful business owner and experienced, serial entrepreneur.

Just as #IWontStarve, #UWontStarve. The journey to becoming a full-time entrepreneur is not easy and yet, with books like *U Won't Starve* in your arsenal, it will make it that much more manageable.

Thank you for joining me on this journey. Let's get started.

Principle #1:
Hustle While You Work

First, let's begin by dispelling a major myth. Hustle While you Work is not the same thing as *hustling*. For some of us, when we think about the word hustling, we think of individuals standing on the corner, or doing something superficial or insignificant to make money. While this can be true, the hustle is also a mindset. Think about it. The hustle should be so in you that it becomes second nature, almost like your default setting. Meaning no matter what developments may be happening in your life or around you, you know you're going to be okay because, as your natural instinct, the hustle will kick in. The hustle is also not about taking advantage of anyone.

Hustling can be anything that involves making money. While the money may be exciting, being a hustler makes it hard for you to focus on one thing.

My first hustle began in high school. At this point, my grandmother had sole custody of me, and she was doing the best she could financially. You see, we didn't ride traditional school buses to school like other places. In order to get to school from my neighborhood, and many other neighborhoods, we had to catch the city bus. This required money, but of course, my grandmother couldn't afford that every day.

I was blessed to have a few family members that worked for NJ Transit. They were able to supply me with bus tickets. Bus tickets were student coupons or mini vouchers if you will. This helped low-income families like mine send their children to school on the city bus. This was very common in my neighborhood. However, I went to school on the other side of town, and those kids' parents didn't have bus tickets to give them. That's when the light bulb went off. My grandmother would get rolls and rolls of them.

One day, I had the bright idea to take more than I needed. I would sell them to the students in my school, who I knew also rode the bus. This put a little money in my pocket and whenever I needed to buy food or snacks, I didn't have to worry about asking her for extra money. Essentially, this was my first job. At that time, I discovered that I had the hustle as a default setting. I was a visionary. Most importantly, I became a problem-solver.

This is the best use of the hustle - solving problems. Whether it's your problems or someone else's past, present, or future problems. In business, Hustle While You Work can mean having a side hustle while you work your full-time job. For a student, it can mean hustling while you're finishing your degree. Lastly, the person preparing for retirement, and getting ready for the next career. No matter what your circumstances are, the hustle is a great tool to use to solve the problem. The *work* portion of this principle is where I tend to lose people because this is the portion that talks about having a plan. Your plan involves the specific steps you are going to take to help you get to your destination.

This first requires a decision. A decision on where you want to go and the path you want to take. To further illustrate this point,

I turn to my famous example of me driving to New York City, leaving my home in Columbia, SC. This is a 12-hour drive, which as you can imagine, is a very long and tedious journey. I use this example because this was a plan I had to make over 100 times in my life and each time was different. Why was the journey different you ask? The journey was different because each time my circumstances were different.

For example, I have taken this trip with $5 or $500 dollars in my pocket. I have driven my own car or hitched a ride. I have taken the bus many times, which added about six hours, or the train, which was about two extra hours. When things were really sweet, I caught a plane, which was only two hours. You get the point. As you can see, the destination never changed nor did my decision to go to New York. The only thing that changed was my circumstances, which would ultimately dictate my plan of action. This determined the work I had to put in to get to my destination.

Hustle While You Work starts with your decision. In my last book, *I Won't Starve,* I wrote that my wife and I were in a bad space. In 2013, she was pregnant with my son, we were behind on bills and trying our best to get caught up. Our daughter was five-years-old at the time, and we had expenses with her as well. You read where I talked about setting up tables at the flea market selling our clothes and DVDs at the barbershop to make ends meet. At this point, I already decided that I would pursue my career in photography, but under these circumstances, I would have to figure out a plan to make this happen.

The first step of my plan was to get a job. If you know me you know I'm a convicted felon, so this wouldn't be anything glamorous. This was cool because I needed something to hold me over until my business took off. I started asking people I knew about opportunities, and the first thing that opened up was a driving position at a dealership for one day a week. It paid $100 the same day, so that worked. I still needed more. After about a month or so, I had a couple of other job options.

A friend of mine called me with an opportunity to work construction with him as a laborer making $12/hour. At the same time, I received a call from one of my church members who knew someone that could get me a job working as a houseman at a hotel for $8/hour. I considered both options. Of course, construction is a well-respected industry. It was certainly more respected than cleaning bathrooms in a hotel. It even *sounds* better, but I chose the hotel job because this fit into my plan of pursuing my career in photography. The job as a houseman was a day job, which meant I would go in at eight in the morning and get off at four in the afternoon. This meant I could still book photography gigs and be at home in the evenings with my family.

I'm happy to say the plan worked. My photography business was growing and not even one year later, I was able to leave my job as a houseman and move into my own office space located in the heart of downtown. As you have been reading through this principle, I hope that through the examples I've shared, you have been enlightened and come to a greater understanding of what it means to Hustle While You Work.

To reiterate, Hustle While You Work is about a few things, but the three most important are, you must have the vision to use your hustle to problem solve, you must make a decision, and you must have a plan. How this plan comes together will look different for everyone. *#UWon'tStarve* was created to be a training guide for three demographics, high school and college students (Gen Z, 1995-2010), Baby Boomers (1946-1964) and Millennials (1981-1994), of which I am considered to be.

Let's start with Gen Z, my student population, (high school and college). While you're in school, your first and primary goal is to get an education. College may have been drilled into your head as the way out of the neighborhood so that you can live a better life. I had the same experience growing up. I was told I was going to college because I needed to leave where I was. College became a way of escape for me. It was the only reason I came to South Carolina.

If college is not in your future, I understand. My goal is to *inspire* you by letting you know that you have other options. Whether or not that future includes college, is up to you, but you have to do something. For high schoolers you're getting prepared for college, for my college students, you are preparing to graduate.

When I arrived in South Carolina to attend Benedict College, I was broke, my paperwork was not in order and I had no family to make sure everything was taken care of. Today I believe more and more students are deciding that college is not the way. Finishing my degree and being one of the first in my family to graduate college was a blessing. While I know that some of you see it this way, I know all of you will not share my same thought process. Entrepreneurship may be a good fit for you. It didn't matter that I graduated college because I had a background. This pretty much guaranteed that I could not ever get a glamorous job as I mentioned before.

Ultimately, here's what I want you to remember:

1. **Your education is your work at this time.** It needs to be taken seriously because it translates to other areas of your life, especially your business.

2. **Develop a skill set.** This is a part of the hustle for you. You can take this opportunity to explore your interests and decide on the direction you want to take.

3. **Start your business on the side.** Get your education and perfect your plan as you work toward becoming a full-time entrepreneur.

To my Baby Boomers, you have been working on your job for 20 years or more and now you are headed towards retirement. This is the time for you to leverage your career or hobbies, to begin exploring entrepreneurship. You have the skills and experiences to be the most effective in this space. It's important to make the decision to start a business and make a plan that will help you transition from your career to your business. What I want to do through this book is to *expose* you to the different options available.

1. **You are the captain of the industry.**
   As you prepare for retirement, this is the time to consider becoming a consultant, pursue certifications, or get additional education in something more aligned in business or your industry. This will get you in the position to have everything in line before your retirement day.

2. **Now is also the time to consider using your hobby (things you do outside of the job), that you have been doing for years to start a business.** This can be anything you do in your spare time right now. You already have the years doing this on the side, now is the time to legitimize and monetize your hobby and turn it into a business you will work full-time after retirement.

3. **Get a new skill.** It's ok to take classes, go back to school, or learn a new trade to work as a business. You have all the time and wisdom of your previous work experience to learn something new and begin a brand-new journey as an

entrepreneur in your, "golden years."

For my millennials, some of you may already be in your career job and married with children. Others of you may have recently graduated from college and are at the beginning of your career. For my career professionals, let's say you've been on this job and in your position for 10 -15 years. You find yourself in a space where you want to pursue something different. Now is the time to pivot, but you may be afraid to because you're unsure of what those next steps will be and more importantly, you've created your entire lifestyle around your job. This will not only require you to *transform* your mindset, but also make the necessary adjustments, so you can be a successful entrepreneur. None of this happens without putting in the work, nor will it happen overnight.

As you hustle while you work, it's important to:

1. **Start working on your gift now and taking it seriously.** Visualize what you want to do outside of your work. Many of you reading this book are very passionate about the business or businesses you've been considering. It's important to have the necessary conversations with your family and take some time to think about how this will impact your current lifestyle.

2. **Make a decision.** Get laser-focused. While you may have experimented with different businesses, this step is

about creating tunnel vision. It's time to focus on the one business you will devote yourself to that will replace the job and not simply the income. In this step you should eliminate all the ideas that have nothing to do with your business. This way you can make the necessary changes to work towards your goal.

3. **Make a plan**. Making a plan can be a few things. Start by giving yourself a timeframe. While on the job, work on your side hustle, to make sure you reach your deadline or targeted date. If your business will require significant lifestyle changes, begin making small changes now to make the transition smoother when you go full-time. This is the time to lay

out everything you want to do so you can successfully execute your hustle into a business.

When I first began my entrepreneurial journey, I had no shoes to step in or blueprint to follow. I was figuring this out as I went along, which meant I made plenty of mistakes and some pretty bad decisions. Each time I became stronger and was able to learn and grow. More than anything, my platform became more stable, putting me in a better position. Things were hard for me, way harder than they had to be I believe, but I'm thankful. If you use this book properly, *#UWontStarve* can be that blueprint for you. You can take the lessons from my life and learn from the experiences I will be sharing with you throughout this book. More importantly, you can take these principles, implement them, and change your life.

Hustle While You Work is only the beginning of the #IWontStarve message. Up next is one of the most important principles of your business - Market Research. Now that you've identified the hustle and have developed your plan, it's time to take the next step.

Principle #2
Market Research

ow many of you when you first saw the title of this principle, instantly thought - he's referring to marketing? Marketing and Market Research are **NOT** the same. Marketing is defined as external awareness. Making *others* aware of your product and service. Market Research is *internal* awareness. This principle is about your business, the service you provide, your capability, and your target audience.

When business owners conduct market research, they are doing it to either learn more about their company or learn more about themselves. When you're first starting out in business - the money, how much someone is willing to pay for your services, can often dictate who you are or the direction of your business. What this does is place us on this hamster wheel where we are constantly chasing the dollar, versus becoming who we should become as entrepreneurs and letting the money come to us.

Now, I'm not saying that you shouldn't go after and get what you deserve, you certainly should - because I do. However, properly using this principle will save you years of trial and error. Market Research is essentially you becoming more internally aware of the target markets that need your product or service and how you're best equipped to serve them.

When big brands are choosing their next retail location, a number of factors are taken into consideration. Where a business chooses to place its retail store has a major impact on its future viability, traffic, and presence. Let's consider luxury retailer *Louis Vuitton* to illustrate this point. The types of goods Louis Vuitton sells; luxury handbags, leather goods, accessories, and apparel at a big-ticket cost, requires that their retail stores are placed in locations where they are easily accessible to their ideal customers.

For example, in the Southeast, there are only five retail locations, Atlanta, Jacksonville, Miami, Charlotte, and Charleston, SC. Louis Vuitton performed market research and determined for a number of reasons to include big business industries, professional sports teams, and high-income earners, that these locations were going to provide their desired outcome.

You may be saying to yourself, *"But, I'm getting ready to launch my business and I don't have a large research and development department, what do I do?"* To get you started, here are a few options for you to consider:

1. **Customers.** Who are your customers? Who are the people you will be serving through your business? What demographic information (i.e., age, gender, organization, or community), do you need to know about them? Having this level of clarity will make sure you are producing a product that will match your target customer. This is called segmentation. Asking the right questions about your ideal customer leads you to the people

who will appreciate your level of superiority.

2. **Location.** Where do you position yourself to be easily accessible to your clients? Will you need a brick and mortar location, mobile or virtual? You need to consider your competition and your customer demographic, so you are properly positioned.

3. **Pricing.** Considering the price of your product or service determines how your business operates. The location you choose, as mentioned in the previous step, will also be a determining factor as you are setting your pricing. For those of you with product-based businesses, what overhead expenses will you

need to cover? What is the market range for the product you will be selling? What will it cost for you to make it? If you are providing a service, what will it cost for you to serve your customer? Will you charge an hourly rate? Does it require you to travel? If it does, how will you factor in that cost? This step is all about concentration. You must know where you will focus your time, money, and resources.

4. **Social media.** Getting your business in front of your target market is vitally important. You must know which platform will provide you with this opportunity. If your current client base lives on Twitter, but you've never been able to maximize the platform, you'll have to make

the adjustments in order to reach them. This could mean hiring someone, getting an intern, or automating your posts using mediums such as Social Oomph or Hootsuite. Choosing the right platform cuts down on the time it takes to gather your market data. Where do your potential clients currently live on social media? What are their go-to platforms? Which platform do you prefer, and which will help you immediately get in front of your target audience?

The options presented above are designed to help you become more internally aware of what you need. Market research is very important, yet most entrepreneurs fail to complete this step. I have found that many take the leap, (launch their business), before making sure their platform is secure. Most entrepreneurs fail to complete this step because this is not the "pretty" side of the business. I mentioned in Hustle While You Work that the "work" portion is where I tend to lose people because the work is oftentimes what entrepreneurs fail to produce.

In full transparency, I never wanted to be a photographer. However, once I decided to take my photography seriously, I dove in headfirst. Once I dove in, I took every photography job imaginable. I was hired to conduct Mother's Day photoshoots, take pictures at children's birthday parties, and even *funerals*. It wasn't until I was hired to take headshots for a local law firm, that I began to get clarity on the type of client I wanted to serve.

I'll never forget that phone call. I remember him asking if I would be interested in taking the headshots for his law firm? I immediately said yes, but I was extremely nervous. When I arrived at his office on the day of the shoot, his staff was very accommodating and allowed me to be as creative as I wanted to be. That was the day I decided I wanted to serve more clients like him.

In order to develop this specialty, I would need to restructure my business. Prior to this, I had only been exploring. Now, I was able to identify my target audience. Sometimes, you have to try different options to see what you want as well as what you don't want. Your specialty or niche should best be determined by default or market research - mine was the latter.

I knew the level of service I was going to provide, and my ideal customer had surfaced. Not only did I find the right environment for my business to flourish. I understood that this was the customer base that would be able to pay me what I felt my talents were worth on a consistent basis.

Once I made the decision, I delved deeper into market research, this time focusing on what I could learn indirectly by using statistics compiled by other organizations. I started with the US Census. I used the Census to find out the number of people in the city of Columbia. At the same time, my wife was working on completing a Google Search to determine if there was a lucrative market for the type of photography services I wanted to provide. I chose Corporate Photography.

Learning that there were only 150,000 people in the city, I knew that there wasn't a lot to work with. However, a subsequent search about local law firms showed promise. As it turns out, there were 400 law firms in Columbia and the majority of them were located in or around the downtown area.

Immediately, my wife began designing the brochures I would need and now that I was armed with this information, it was time for me to hit the streets. I decided I would drive downtown, park, walk into these law firms, and introduce myself and my services. Finding out that the majority of these offices were located downtown, I knew my next decision was to get an office space. Because most of the law firms were located downtown, we decided this is where my office would go. Again - location. Having an office downtown made me easily accessible to my clients. Many of them would come to get their headshots taken on their lunch break and I was easily a 10-minute walk for most.

In summary, here are the four points I want you to remember:

1. Specialization - Identify the product, service, customer, market, or area of technology you specialize in. Your specialization can be determined by default or market research.

2. Differentiation - How are you different? What is your competitive advantage? Your area of excellence, superiority, and your unique selling proposition?

3. Segmentation - Who are the customers? Who is most appreciative of your area of superiority? What are their demographics? (Things you can observe from the outside). What are their psychographics? (What is their current lifestyle? What motivates them? What are their aspirations)? How would you describe your perfect customer?

4. Concentration - Where you focus your time, money & resources. What are the best possible ways to contact your ideal customer? What is the best possible media? How do you appeal to their pain points?

At its core, Market Research is any effort that helps you better understand your business and potential customers—their preferences and behaviors. I've assembled a list of the best market research methods you can use during this process:

Method	Purpose
Focus Groups	Bringing together groups of potential or current customers to gather insights into their preferences, behaviors, and purchasing patterns.
Interviewing	One-on-one research sessions to dig deeper into the consumer's psychology.
Observational Research	Studying the behavior of consumers in real-world settings.

Method	Purpose
User-Behavior Tools	Tools for studying how users interact with your products or services.
Market Research Data & Statistics Analysis Tools	Databases that can give you broader insights into market trends. (i.e., US Census, SBA (Small Business Administration), SCORE (Service Corps of Retired Executives), and Small Business Development Center (SBDC)

Principle #3
Doing Business on Your Own Level

This principle is personal. I remember when I first started out in business. I was a young college student who had no problem hustling, but I knew that that could only take me so far. While in college, I became a felon. All of the time I spent in college, attending classes, and working on my GPA, would not matter when I graduated. Because of my record, I knew I wouldn't be able to get a career job, but it wouldn't be because I didn't try. I applied for jobs. I went on job interviews and even received job offers. And with every job offer came the background check and ultimately, the rejection. After experiencing my share of rejection, I decided to become a full-time entrepreneur.

These days, entrepreneurship has become the new wave. Everybody who is somebody has or wants to start a business. However, when I decided to become an entrepreneur, it wasn't nearly as popular. We were looked at as lazy or radical, especially, being a college student at an HBCU (Historically Black College or University). The instructors, who are mostly Baby Boomers, believed that I should wait my turn, I wasn't old enough to start a business, and that my degree was more important. I didn't understand that then, but I do now. Let's be clear, I totally disagree.

However, I understand that they were only giving me the information that was given to them. That is why this principle is so important. This principle is all about you. Everybody's story is different, and everyone has their own path, so what you define as *Doing Business on Your Own Level,* will always be unique. Nevertheless, I can promise you one thing, starting a business is not an easy task, no matter what you see on social media.

Some of you are of the perception that in order to become an entrepreneur and step out and do business, you have to be in a particular place financially. Or, you have to have gained a certain level of knowledge prior to launching. This is not true. When I first started my cleaning business, I had $500, which purchased my flyers, minimal supplies, and business licenses. Within one month of handing out flyers and word-of-mouth advertising, I was able to secure my first residential cleaning job. I didn't have much money and didn't know much about the cleaning business.

However, I got started where I was and with what I had and four years later, it had become a six-figure commercial cleaning company. You can start wherever you are and grow your way into success. Everyone is not able to begin a business with thousands of dollars in the bank. This may take you a little longer or make things a little harder, but that's okay. The great thing about business is that we all don't have to start on a particular level, but we do have to get started.

As I said before, this looks different for everybody. Let's explore how this relates to our three target demographics.

For my Gen Zers, you may be in college or have recently graduated high school. This can be a very confusing time. Everyone has an idea of what you should be doing, and the expectations that come with your decisions don't seem to make things any clearer. Most people aren't telling you to be an entrepreneur. If you are graduating high school, the advice is to go to college, join the military, or get a job.

If you're in college, the advice is to pursue your career, find stable employment, or get an Advanced degree. All of this is fine, these are examples of the **WORK** portion of Hustle While You Work. Entrepreneurship is a lifestyle. For the rest of your life, you have to see opportunities where others see problems. You'll be the one who is the problem solver and use whatever resources you have, to start your business, or innovate something that will change the dynamic of your life.

For example, you're in school and realize you need some extra money, and you know how to cut grass. However, you don't have any money to start a landscaping business or buy any equipment. This would be a problem for everyone else. However, you live a lifestyle that tells you there is always away. This means that you are willing to ask someone to cut their grass with their equipment. You're willing to line up four jobs this week and get deposits upfront so that you could have enough to rent the equipment. No matter what the problem is, you're of the mindset that there is a solution.

To my Baby Boomers, at the time this book is being written, the youngest Baby Boomer is 56 years young. You've already been on your job for at least 15 years and are about five to 10 years away from retirement. By now, you have found out that everything they told you was a lie. You were told that you would live forever. You were told that you would survive a nuclear attack and that you would have Social Security to fall back on, and every day you get up for work, you know that's not true.

I have news for you, all is not lost. You're still relevant and you're still needed. Baby Boomers are known for being trustworthy and loyal. You have a commitment to family and your community. Your dedication to the workforce has been unmatched. I truly believe that it takes a great employee to be a great entrepreneur. For years, you've been counted on to open and close the business every day and train and supervise new employees as they came in. You're ready! Ready as you will ever be.

While you've been working on your job, you may have had interests you have not pursued. Maybe you've always wanted to open a daycare because you love children. Or you've always wanted to launch an event planning business because you enjoy setting up events. Or, you've dreamed about becoming a corporate consultant, but in your mind, you thought you had to be in a certain position **before** you made that happen. You can start your business today, right where you are, with what you currently have.

Lastly, millennials, as I talk to y'all, I'm talking to myself. We are probably the most talked-about generation of all. Let's be clear, it's not all good talk. We are considered the most educated and also the most likely to live at home with our parents. This doesn't have to be our legacy. We have the world at our fingertips, we only have to believe in ourselves and most importantly, each other.

In a perfect world, the principles in this book would've gone in order. However, that is not the case. I started with this principle doing business on your own level. When I started my photography business, all I had was my camera. I was already taking pictures and as it turns out, that was all I needed. My wife and I were hurting financially, however, I didn't allow that to hold me back. I used all I had to get started right where I was in the current state we were in. The rest came later.

What does this mean to you? Some of us are on the job of our dreams or so we thought. Some of us may be on job number three. And maybe some of us *are* still living with our parents. We all have a story, and whatever that may be for you, it still puts you in a position to get started on creating your new legacy as an entrepreneur.

We are the workforce generation that has the most available to us and yet we are doing the least. We have the most education. We have the most opportunities. And we are wasting it because the time we think we have, we don't. Somehow, we find ourselves waiting on the perfect moment. The perfect conversation. The perfect opportunity and the perfect financial backing to start our business. Everything that you need to start, you already have.

This principle is for those of us who have the mindset that they need to drive a certain car, live a certain lifestyle, or have a certain amount of money in the bank to become an entrepreneur.

When it comes to doing business on your own level, I want you to remember these three things:

1. **There is never a perfect time to start a business.** Some people spend their whole life waiting for the right moment. Don't make this mistake. The moment you get the idea for the business or the moment the opportunity presents itself is the

right time. Things change every day, and with that, goes opportunity. Have you ever heard the phrase, "Here today gone tomorrow?" This is a very true statement. Here's another one I like. "Stay ready so you don't have to get ready."

All this means is that you have to always be mentally prepared for your time to come. I emphasize mental, because that's what entrepreneurship is, a mindset! As I stated before, it's a lifestyle, one you will never be able to turn off.

2. **You have what you need to get started.** This is one of the biggest traps of all. Your friends, family, society at large, and of course, social media, made you believe that you

had to have this imaginary list of accomplishments before you take the first step into entrepreneurship. Don't fall for this trap. Whether you have $5 or $500 dollars. Whether you have 10 men or you're a solo act. I promise you; you have all you need. The day you decided to see the solutions in everyone's problems. That moment you chose to see the glass half full, instead of half empty. That night when everyone thought you were out of options and you made a way out of no way. It was then that the dispute was settled. You have more than you need.

3. **Become an independent contractor.** One of the key benefits of being an entrepreneur is the sense of

freedom. The ability to call your own shots and be your own boss. However, one of the biggest responsibilities is to be someone else's boss. This is a commitment that a lot of people run from and for good reason. Especially, if you're not prepared. If this is you, I recommend that you become an Independent Contractor. This would give you the freedom you want without the extra added responsibility. A great example of this is Truck Drivers, Plumbers, Electricians, and of course, Photographers. You get my point. These individuals have unlimited earning potential without that other responsibility. At least, not at the beginning. This gives them a chance to get prepared for full-time entrepreneurship on their own terms. Not a bad deal!

Principle #4
Networking
(Be the Cheese)!

When you think of networking, I am sure the first thing that comes to mind is attending a Happy Hour or after-work social event. While there's nothing particularly wrong with participating in these types of functions, it can be difficult for networking to happen in these spaces. First, networking is not attending a Happy Hour event enjoying half-priced food or drinks. After all, how much business conversation can you have after you've had a few glasses of wine or a few bottles of beer?

The networking I'm talking about is when you purposely go out and align yourself with the people and companies you want to do business with. In this principle, I'm going to break down my approach to networking by challenging you to shift your mindset about what networking is. When it comes to networking, it's important to put yourself in situations where you can be seen for your business. This can be done in a variety of ways even if you don't like being in large crowds or the center of attention.

Well you may say, "I'm an introvert and I don't perform well in large crowds." I hear this a lot when I'm coaching or training. This is one of the first steps to maximizing your approach to networking. Let's take a look at extroverts and introverts,
which one are you?

Extroverts	Introverts
Enjoy being the center of attention	Don't enjoy being the center of attention
Gain energy from being around other people	Prefer quiet spaces
Outgoing and enthusiastic	Quiet and reserved
Tend to think out loud	Deeply focused
Have large social networks	Desires close one-on-one relationships

Regardless of whether you are an introvert or extrovert, it's important to have a plan when it comes to networking. What does that look like? My method is called **"BEING THE CHEESE!"** This was inspired by a Gary Vee story referring to a person selling cheese at a wine festival. If you're familiar with wine festivals, then you'll know that there could be hundreds of vendors, wine companies from all over, and people coming from far and wide to taste the wine. You will also know that the only food is usually **THE CHEESE!** The person selling the cheese had no competitors, only customers.

How do you become the cheese in your business? You need to activate the first three principles in this book:

Hustle While You Work - Putting this principle into play will help you build the confidence you need when going out. You can use this as your practice time. This is the time for you to perfect your craft and build your skill level. When the time comes for you to present your business at a networking event, you can confidently speak to what you have to offer and why you're the best candidate to get someone's business.

Market Research - As you would recall in this principle, it's about being internally aware. With the proper market research, you are able to find out where your ideal customer is and will be. Let's go back to my man with the cheese. He knew by attending this wine festival, he was positioning himself to where everybody was his customer and not his competition, to include the wine vendors and individual patrons. This will allow him to maximize his opportunity to promote and sell his product.

Doing Business on Your Own Level - If you're starting out in business, then chances are you may have limited resources, i.e., funds and connections. This doesn't mean that you shouldn't look for networking opportunities. Instead, take the time to research and look for low cost or free opportunities where your market will be and approach them there. Don't be discouraged. Providing a service for free or donating products is another opportunity to get you in the door. Lastly, you can utilize social media.

Social media provides free or low-cost networking opportunities, especially in groups. There are groups created for various interests and there is one for your specific industry. No matter your platform choice, you can still be the cheese and place yourself specifically where your ideal customer will be.

When it comes to networking, remember this:

1. **Be aware.** It is important to be aware of yourself and your business. Having this awareness allows you to be very targeted for your intended result. Being focused prevents you from being all over the place when it comes to networking, especially on social media. Social media is not a bad thing, but it is important to use it properly.

2. **Your appearance.** It is important that you are dressed appropriately for the business you own and the

potential client you are meeting. For example, if you are meeting with bankers, lawyers, and high-level executives and if you have a professional business, i.e., a marketing firm or financial planning, you would want to dress in business attire. Suits may be required, but only where appropriate.

If you have another type of business, graphic design for example, it is appropriate for you to wear a nice, clean polo shirt with your company name or logo with slacks or jeans. Being aware of your target client and your business, helps you make a great first impression. Another branding lesson is to always have clothing that promotes your company. Make sure you are always representing.

Your business card design also plays a huge role in this because they are a part of your appearance. I'll forever be known as the guy with the small business card. For years, my business card was a small 2 x 2, where most traditional designs were 3 x 2. See the difference?

Investing in the design and printing of your business cards will make sure they are memorable and stand out. There are a lot of options now that will not cost hundreds of dollars as they once did. Be creative. Put some thought into it.

3. **The Magic is in the Follow-Up.** It is my business practice to follow up fast. Usually this means within the first 24-48 hours after meeting someone. These follow-ups are designed to keep me at the forefront of the mind of the business contact and to see how I can be of service.

Remember, most people would have received at least 20-30 business cards when you met them. Being the cheese, having a memorable business card, and following up, is a sure way for you to stay at the forefront of their mind.

Principle #5
Strategic
Alliances/Partnerships

Just as with Doing Business on Your Own Level, this principle is also personal. When I was in the early phases of my business, I spent a lot of those years perfecting my craft and building my skill level. It wasn't until I had been doing business for a while that I recognized the need and importance of having strategic partners. I imagine that if you are in the startup phase as I was, you also focused on the same thing, working and building, making sure your business's foundation is strong. Even with this in mind, the reality is that none of us can do business alone.

That's why this principle is important, because it is the key that can unlock the next level of your business - strategic partnerships. It's also why this principle is placed at the end it is the last in a series of processes to help you become a successful entrepreneur.

Before we get to strategic partnerships, let's define partnerships. When it comes to *partnerships*, there are pros and there are cons. The pros are, they can provide more access to capital, you are able to bring different skill sets to the table and third you get an opportunity to receive a level of support from a partner through shared ideas and shared risk.

The cons of partnerships are the following: accountability. Some entrepreneurs don't want to have to answer to anyone. The second reason is friction. Friction is what happens when there is no equality of duties, funds, or time. The third reason is liability. With partnerships, you are liable for another person's actions. Can you trust this person to conduct themselves as they are supposed to? In a partnership, your assets are exposed to greater risk.

I can understand why it would be difficult for individuals to take on a partnership. However, you can only get so far by yourself. You need allies. You need people outside of the four walls of your business that have your best interest at heart. If you've been trying to do business alone, I want you to know that there is a better way. That way is creating strategic partnerships.

So, how do I define strategic partnerships? Before I get to the definition, first, let's dispel a few myths. A strategic partnership is not a business structure. Nor does it have to be legally binding. I define a strategic partnership as a business tactic. Strategic partnerships are about building human capital. It is employing forces, the entities, organizations, and individuals you will strategically align yourself with, for the purposes of accomplishing a goal or completing a project.

Many entrepreneurs see partnerships as lifetime, permanent arrangements, or marriages. These alliances are not bound by covenant. You can create a one-time strategic partnership opportunity and it does not have to go any further than that.

When it comes to strategic alliances, you should consider partnering with the following:

1. **A civilian** - This is not a random individual. It should be someone that complements what you have been able to do and build. Someone that can join you in your efforts, and who you are able to strategically align your business with.

2. **A fellow entrepreneur** - It is a great idea to partner with fellow entrepreneurs who have been able to make connections you can utilize and vice versa.

3. **Business entity** - Sometimes you can create a strategic alliance with an organization. This can vary

depending on your business. Examples of this are government agencies, non-profit organizations, or corporations.

4. **Banks** - No matter the stage of your business, you will always need financial support via information, access to programs, and other resources. Banks are the center of every community it makes sense for all facets of your business to build a strategic alliance with a financial institution.

You might be wondering when is the best time to look for strategic partners?

a. **When you have gone as far as you can go on your own.** Initially, when you get started in business, you work really hard to keep your business afloat, which means all of your energy, time, and effort goes into building. At some point, you will get tired of bumping your head against the wall or feeling as if you have reached a ceiling. When this happens, it's time to consider strategic alliances to help open other doors for you.

b. **When you realize you don't have everything you need to move your business forward.** As you're building your business, you will come to the realization that you are missing essential core components. Right now, this might not be important, but as you continue to grow, this moment will come. To help guide your thought process to the right time, let's look at a test you can perform to assess the health of your business.

Business Diagnostic. In the beginning of your business, you would have already completed your SWOT Analysis - I hope, which focuses on the state of your business as a whole. Now it is time to complete a business diagnostic. This diagnostic is to help you identify the specific pain point that is preventing you from moving forward. For example, when your car needs repair, it begins to make a noise. You may hear a knock in the engine, or it doesn't start at all. In order to really identify the problem, you need to get a diagnostic test.

The diagnostic lets you know specifically what needs repair. Depending on the nature of the problem, you may need to hire a professional. So, it is with your business. There are some problems you can fix in your business, but for those you can't - it is best to connect with someone you can form a strategic alliance with, to get the help you need.

Here are some questions you need to ask yourself:

What's missing (i.e. money, resources, information, or connections)?

Who in my network can I connect with to fill the void in my business?

Answering these questions will help you identify who you need to connect with, i.e., a civilian, fellow entrepreneur, business entity, or bank?

After you have identified when you need to find strategic partners, your next question should be *how* do I find them? Let's go back to networking. If you have been successful in your efforts, then you would have already connected with individuals and organizations that could be your ideal partners. Networking is not only designed to help you find customers who will buy your products, but also make strategic alliances and positive connections.

My advice is to do the following:

a. **Pay attention to your clients and customers.** Identify their areas of weakness and insert yourself as a problem solver or assess where you can add value. Gaining this knowledge puts you in a position of strength.

b. **Supporting Others.** This should come from a genuine place. Support can be shown in multiple ways and displays your level of commitment to your potential partner. Place yourself in a position to show up and help others. Again, go back to networking. There is nothing wrong with providing a discounted product or free service to show your support and that you believe in someone else's ideals.

Side note: Some strategic alliances will be mutually beneficial like a traditional partnership. Both parties could walk away from the partnership with their business in a better position. And sometimes only one partner is able to benefit initially. Knowing their pain points as well as yours can present a clear proposal when you make your pitch.

An ideal strategic partnership can be filled with sharing, benefits, cooperation, and information. Let's start with sharing:

a. **Sharing.** This step is about willingness. It's important to find someone willing to share information, ideas, and tactics to help you move your business forward.

b. **Benefits.** You should choose to form a strategic alliance with someone you can connect with that is able to be of benefit to you. The goal is to find the missing pieces to your puzzle. The benefits don't always have to be monetary. As we mentioned earlier, this can be someone who has access to information, connections, or resources that you don't have.

c. **Cooperation** - These individuals will work on your behalf even when you aren't around. This can look like entering your name as a candidate for opportunities when they come across their desk. They are willing to speak up for you and your business in their circles. Most importantly, they're emotionally invested in the growth and development of you and your business.

d. **Information** - This is probably the most important of all. As an entrepreneur, it's difficult to function without information, especially pertinent information.

Some of the best resources are individuals you might not expect, such as administrative and janitorial staff and security guards. These people know more about the company than the CEO. They are the inspiration for the quote, "Treat everyone the same from the CEO to the janitor." More often than not, these people hold the keys to the castle, and it comes in the form of valuable information.

While the above-mentioned steps are about you and your potential strategic partner, you should always be willing to put in the work yourself. In saying this, there is a science to creating strategic partnerships. Before we go any further, let's remember that strategic partnerships:

1. **Are not permanent.** This is not to be confused with the business structure, where you have to remain in it for the length of time that the business is in existence. Nor are you responsible for the negative decisions that the other party makes. This is one of the myths that prevent most beginner entrepreneurs from making successful strategic alliances.

2. **Not legally binding.** Most people say that partnerships are like a marriage. This may be true in most cases. However, in order to achieve a successful strategic partnership, you are not required to be legally bonded to anyone. Like a marriage, this is a give and take relationship, but when it's

over you are free to go with no strings attached.

3. **Execution.** This is referring to any task or project that you are not capable of completing on your own, or with your company resources. These tasks require the help of a strategic partner to ensure proper execution.

So, what does this look like for you?

1. **For my Gen Zers** - Now is the perfect time to partner with a friend who has the book smarts while you have the skill set. You may have never wanted to go to college, but you've been working hard since high school. Your hard work and industry knowledge, coupled with your

friend's formal education, can be the beginning of a great strategic alliance.

If you're in college, this is the perfect time to build human capital and network because chances are, you'll be meeting people from all walks of life. Your graduating class will be filled with men and women who will go on to become investment bankers, realtors, corporate executives, and successful entrepreneurs in their own right.

2. **For my Millennials -** We have the largest workforce demographic, and the most education. However, with all of this going for us, we haven't grasped the concept of collaboration. We were taught to be

skeptical of one another and this has affected our ability to grow as entrepreneurs. Our strength lies in our ability to collaborate and share our gifts and talents, wherever you look, you have a counterpart in some high-paying job or government position. We may be on the job, following the footsteps of our parents, however, they truly wanted more for us. They wanted us to explore and conquer the world. Alone we have a hard time seeing our way, but together we can create the way.

3. **Baby Boomers** - Out of all of the generations, you are in the best position. At this stage, you have had the opportunity to make vital contacts and/or develop important

relationships throughout your entire career. You are trusted and respected in your position because of the longevity in your industry, which puts you in a position of strength. You are automatically seen as more credible and individuals are more likely to want to partner with you. It is imperative that you do the best you can to nurture those relationships or plant seeds to make it easier for you to transition from employee to entrepreneur when you retire.

While you've been working on your job for the last 20 years, you have been able to make relationships with individuals in other departments in your company as well as outside vendors. Now that you are close to retirement and about to launch your business, those same relationships you have built, you can use them now to help you as you build your business. This can lead to future contracts or the formation of a strategic alliance.

U Won't Starve

For me, writing *U Won't Starve*, was a true labor of love. When I started *I Won't Starve*, it was more involved, and it was definitely all about me. I know a lot of people thought that *I Won't Starve* was going to be what *U Won't Starve* is about and that is giving some tips about entrepreneurship. However, I had to write *I Won't Starve* first, to get a lot of demons out that I had and share all the things that happened prior to this. *I Won't Starve* was a personal journey of mine, not just about the things I've learned over the last seven to eight years in business.

Writing that book really freed me. I thought for me, it was the perfect time for me to give it to other individuals. It's been hell, or at least I thought at the time, but I understand that what I went through was extremely necessary. Also, I feel that it's even more necessary to make sure that the people that follow behind me don't have to go through the same hardships that I did.

As a result, I created *five* principles. These are the five principles that I used to get ahead and put me in a position to get to where I am today. I started talking about Hustle While You Work back in 2013. If you read my first book, then you'll remember that in 2013, my wife and I were eating from Harvest Hope Food Bank. This is how we shopped for groceries every week. If you're not from South Carolina, you may not be familiar with Harvest Hope, it's like the Salvation Army. Every week, families are able to come and get groceries, diapers, and other non-perishable items for their homes.

My wife lost her job and I was barely working, so we did what we had to do. I didn't know where my next work opportunity was coming from and all I had was my camera. I already said I was going to take this seriously and create a business out of it. However, with all this happening, it was very tempting to put it to the side again like I did the year prior. Only this time, I decided to really focus on it and use the resource that was at my disposal. I understood that I didn't have enough money to go out and do this by myself. I needed to have some concrete income to pay my bills. When I started looking for jobs and got presented with two options, I always kept in mind my decision. I was determined to become a full-time photographer.

With that in mind as I wrote in the book, *I Won't Starve* about how I took an $8 an hour job, I always had the end in mind. I knew that this was only to get me over the hump, to take care of the family, and make sure that we had our bills covered. I worked my behind off every day at work and outside of work, perfecting my craft, and learning everything needed to learn in order to get better and grow at a rapid pace. My business grew in no time and then, I started making great alliances. I started understanding more about the business and more about what I actually wanted to do with my business.

This is when the market research portion comes in. My goal was to do this full-time. I wondered what was going to pay me enough money to take care of my family. You know, it was cool doing a party here and there and doing this event and that event, but I really needed to know that if I left my job was it going to sustain me and my family? And then I figured out that it was going to be corporate and commercial photography, only it didn't happen overnight. As soon as I figured it out, I immediately put things in motion. I stepped out on my own level where I was and got an office.

I got my office a little over a year after I took the job or literally right at the year mark. I still didn't leave immediately. It took about five months before I actually quit my job. I got an office right downtown in the heart of the business community, which put me in a position to take on the customers and the client base that I wanted to work with after that. It was time to let them know about me and this is where networking came in. I understood where all my people were. I went out there and found them. I went in and put myself in the place where they were.

I still didn't have a lot of money at the time because I wasn't making a lot. However, whatever was cheap or free or right at $100, I was there. I was there until I was able to grow. Once I grew, I found out that in order to keep going to another level, you have to have contracts. It was one thing to get one-off jobs, but I knew I needed to have a contract. I needed the people to call me on a regular basis. I asked myself, "Who can do that here?"

This is when I started going from law office to law office, to the city, to the county and to other different municipalities who had the resources to be able to carry me and my family for a long time. I started networking with them. I was networking and attending their functions. I put myself out there and around them. Just like everything else, it started off slow. These were tester jobs. You know, we'll try you here, can you take headshots for this office? Can you shoot this banquet or this function? These were the jobs I had to be willing to do before they were willing to commit to me. Once I won them over and they got a chance to see my work, I was good to go.

I was excited about the opportunities and they were coming in fast. After a short while, I realized I was reaching the proverbial glass ceiling. Once I got to the ceiling and the contracts weren't coming in as fast as I would have liked them to, or I know that they didn't have much more to offer me. I asked myself the following questions, how can I grow? How can I get better?

I started reverse-engineering the resources from those same people who gave me jobs. I knew they had other alliances that they could put me in contact with. I also knew they had connections to people that they could put me in contact with. While I knew that, I started figuring out how I can be of service to them enough for them to help and introduce me. This put me in front of the other people that I needed to be in front of, to help me grow. This is where the strategic alliances and strategic partnerships came into play. This has truly worked for my business.

I know it's a mouthful, but all that happened in a four-year time frame. I went from working an $8 hour job to being a six-figure earner. This is when I realized I had a system in place that worked. I actually worked the system, and I got results in no time.

It took a long time for me to find this out. At the time that this book was being written, I had been an entrepreneur for 20 years. If I would have known this, it would have taken me less time to grow in business. But now I'm able to continue to duplicate the same process with other businesses that I've created and it works tremendously fast as long as you follow the steps.

My goal was to put the steps out here for you guys and to put you in a situation that you didn't have to go through all of it alone. I went through all the hardships in the past. Listen, you can't skip steps, you are going to have your own issues. I feel as though it is my responsibility to step in to shed light on the issues that I went through so that you can focus on the ones that you are going to have yourself.

Some of you are going to read this book and you are going to use these principles. For others, you will read this book and already be two principles in. That's fine. That's a blessing, however, you still have to work. I'm a living testimony. At one point, I started to read books by other authors, and they were saying the same things that I'm giving you. The difference is the way they were saying it, it's as if they were speaking in a different language. Oftentimes, that language would be written over someone's head.

This is what inspired me to write this book. I am talking to the person who's coming off of the porch. I decided that I was going to focus on three age brackets of individuals, that I determined were going to be my target audience.

I wanted to work with Gen Zers because again, this is really personal to me. I started my first business at 19, on my 19th birthday. I didn't have anybody to tell me what the real deal was back in those days. As I mentioned earlier, entrepreneurship is the new wave. However, it wasn't even a fad back then. If you jumped out and started a business, then to other people this meant that you were lazy. Because of this, no one was trying to tell me how to do it right. And if they would have, who knows? I probably would have been rich a long time ago. It is my job to go ahead and give you this information.

For my millennials, that's me, we will be the smartest community with a large generation in the workforce. We don't know as much as we think we know, and then what we find out, is that we don't know a lot at all. We are the most educated, but also the most underachieved and it's because we don't do the work.

We don't use the resources that we have at our disposal and some of that we have to blame on our parent and the people that came before us. Don't forget that we have total control and we're raising other generations right now. We have to do a better job of leaving something for them and that starts with entrepreneurship.

Lastly, the baby boomers. This was the largest generation prior to us Millennials. You guys are in control of everything. You are the ones that are in the know, and you have all the skills. You guys have all the knowledge, all the resources, and are the most trusted in the community.

Yet, you are still bitter because you found out that you were lied to. Social Security is not going to be the Savior as they told you. You were told that you were going to live forever. Because of this, you might have decided that you are going to standstill. However, we need you now more than ever to continue to lead us in the right way. It's not too late for you. If you go ahead and take all that knowledge, all the skill set, and couple that with the old school tactics of being respectful and knowing how to conduct business properly, you can still move our community forward even in this age, day, and time.

I wanted to focus on those three communities and the individuals who make up those age groups because I felt like these are the people that are going to be affected by what we have going on for years to come.

Thank you all again for your participation in reading this book. If you have gotten this far, then this means you've already reached the end. I pray that you enjoyed the content.

This is my second baby. I had so much fun producing this content for you guys and I can say that I am truly bitten by the "book bug." More than anything, I really wanted to continue to communicate with my community this way and in this fashion. I want you to celebrate with me with this book because this is information that's going to take you to another level.

Not only is it going to take you higher, but it is also going to take me higher. It's taking me higher by getting it out to you and it's going to take you higher by taking in this information putting it to good use in your life and business venture. I appreciate all you've done.

Thank you so much for taking the first step in trying to grow yourself and your business career.

I love y'all. Peace.

Meet J Haleem

J Haleem Washington is a nationally published, award-winning photographer, established entrepreneur, author, corporate trainer, and motivational speaker. J Haleem was born and raised in Newark, New Jersey. While in college, Jamar pursued many ventures that allowed him to nurture his love for owning and managing businesses. J Haleem started his first business at 19 years old. This birthed the businessman we know today. With more than 20 years of experience as an entrepreneur; he now owns a few businesses and he is able to enjoy his passion for entrepreneurship and training start-up business owners.

AUTHOR

In J Haleem's first book, *I Won't Starve,* he shares his life's experiences, and the highs and the lows that not only comes from dealing with life as a convicted felon but also with owning and operating a business. In a very bold way, J Haleem gives you an intimate look behind the veil as he shares his story from making $8 an hour to running a successful business.

MOTIVATIONAL SPEAKER

J Haleem uses his own personal experiences to motivate & connect with audiences on a variety of platforms. He motivates individuals with challenged backgrounds, on how they can TRANSFORM their skill sets into business ownership opportunities. He INSPIRES aspiring entrepreneurs to transition to becoming full-time business owners. Lastly, His message EXPOSES his audience to the reality that they have the power to transition from surviving to thriving.

CORPORATE TRAINER

J Haleem is a corporate trainer and program developer with many years of experience providing outstanding programs for hundreds of small business owners. He has been in the corporate training field for many years and is known for his dynamic, motivating, and relatable speaking style. J Haleem has delivered business development workshops, which include Market Research, Strategic Partnerships, Sales, and Entrepreneur Development, as well as helping to create and manage programs for local & state municipalities.

BUSINESS COACH

If you seek clear direction, J Haleem can help you and your team determine objectives, set goals and accurately monitor performance, motivate and encourage team members, identify and meet people's needs, understand how personality types interact, and build quality relationships. Whether he is coaching one-on-one or training a corporate, government, or non-profit organization, J Haleem's purpose is to facilitate movement... significant movement. A key part of why individuals hire a coach is to hear the coach's opinion about the client's goals, situation, problems, dynamics, or lifestyle.

Connect with J Haleem

To connect with J Haleem, please visit the following channels:

www.jhaleem.com

For booking and additional information:
info@jhaleem.com

Follow @iamjhaleem on all social media platforms

Subscribe on YouTube:
www.youtube.com/JHaleemTV

Made in the USA
Middletown, DE
18 June 2020